CREATIVE
WHISPERS

JEANNINE GINGRAS

PAGE PUBLISHING
Conneaut Lake, PA

First originally published by Page Publishing 2022

ISBN 978-1-6624-5666-4 (pbk)
ISBN 978-1-6624-5667-1 (digital)

Printed in the United States of America

CONTENTS

REFLECTIONS

Sitting, reflecting a long life spent
Glory, honor, not in the spin
Has life been full as should be
Or a life with regret, continues inside me

To gather facts, welcome results
Face life's challenges without doubt
Being happy, efforts saddened with knots
To be happy, not letting struggles put out

The lives that come forward help
Not all will be with you through the results
The chosen you know, strong smiles and bonds
Also remember, God sent them around

To cherish, accept daily task
A gift from heaven, walking a path
Open your eyes to the people you meet
Let them inside the heart that you seek

Reflections, long time spent
Has come to a circle we all can accept
With hearts that are open, welcoming sounds
Helping with outcome, life with a smile

Letting in happiness
A heart full of love
Can carry us through
A life without doubt

8

THE EYES OF GOD

The eyes of the beholder
They always speak
Or is it the mirrors
False reflection you see

Love yourself, as the one you are
Find the beauty inside, your inner thaw
Letting a hurt become reality
Life is not what you see

Holding the pain, letting it go
Bring back the beauty that you behold
Taking away the beauty as told
Can make a tree stand alone

What you see within your eyes
Is only a part of God's plan
Welcome your talent, letting it shine
A guiding strength in God's hands

Throw away the mirror that cripples your mind
Find the person you have inside
As told by people who see who you are
This person (will) only shine

Forgetting the past can help you stand tall
Young children of hurt can disappear now
With spiritual help, you've always passed
Let them guide you through your life's regrets

Helping of others, the world can be wronged
Guiding a person, holding on strong
A miracle happens to the human race
Releasing the hurt you seem to embrace

Letting it go, the hardest of task
The bulling gone with strength that's unrest
A lifetime of hurt, a sorrowful sight
It's time to let go, help welcome the light

TICK, TOCK, TICK

The time is clicking faster than we think
Tick, tock, tick, tock, tick

To the music of past and present
Time spent, time still to come

With memories of past
Heartaches of tomorrow

Smiles of today
Tears of yesteryear

A gesture of kindness
A striking of hatefulness

The comfort of your home
The disarray of a disaster

The wonders of life
The sorrows of generations lost

The days of dating
The years of blessedness

We always knew
We would grow old

As we watch the clock go
Tick, tock, tick, tock, tick

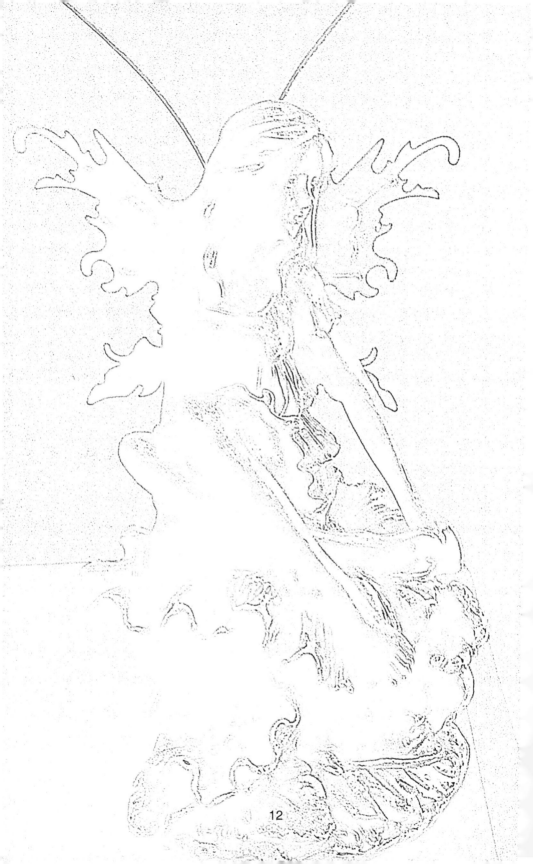

12

Shining Journey

A smile engaging,
Sweetness scent.
Words of wisdom,
Strong in strength.

Sorrowful tears appear each day,
Comfort feelings on display.
Life goes on, strength that's found,
Days go by, nights so long.

I close my eyes, I find your smile,
A comfort I can't live without.
My dreams are far, few between,
I miss you so, please bring me peace.

I long for arms you shared with strength,
To wrap me in your warm embrace.
To laugh and cry, exchange our words,
To shop and figure out our world.

You've traveled to a place of peace,
With beauty that surrounds.
I'll join you someday with a smile,
Once my work on earth is done.

God's embrace will help me through,
The misery of losing you.
Knowing that someday we'll meet,
Together in his love complete.

Wings to carry into flight,
Warmth, wisdom, strength, delight,
God's embracing arms of love,
Into heaven's perfect light.

14

MY ROSARY BEADS

My rosary beads
I keep so near
Inside my purse
Where they are dear

I bring them with me every day
To remind me of my need to pray
If ever they would disappear
My life would not be quite as clear

Of all the blessing I still have
To bring my love so I can share
All the riches I have found
The richness that I feel is proud

You cannot see it, touch, or smell
But you can feel it all around
The peacefulness that does surround
Your inner being's peaceful sounds

My rosary beads
I keep so near
Inside my purse
Always so dear

16

WHERE IS SHE

Where is the girl she used to know?
Where is the girl she could have been?
Has she been lost on the back road of life?
Has she been lost in a world not her own?

Who is she, the person looking in?
Why is she standing alone?
Why does she feel so alone and afraid,
With people so close, yet so far away?

Does she know the reason her tears can't be seen?
Does she know why her cries can't be heard?
How can she live life without herself?
How can she join in as the doors become closed?

Where is she? Will she open her eyes?
Realizing she's been standing in a lie,
Living in someone else's dreams.
Her dream's a fog in her mind.

Will she ever find the strength
To reveal her soul?
Always walking in a shadow
Not of her own.

Roses from Life Within

The smell of roses comes within
The heart that we must carry
The sound of love is further in
The sound that once was buried

The rainbow shines within a distance
Far beyond control
To whisper many secrets
That a body cannot hold

The stars that flutter through the sky
To make the morning bright
Can sometimes form a shadow
Among the morning light

The strength that comes within these scenes
Have carried many thoughts
Of how you are to cherish
A human that is not

So be aware of all there is
To follow you this day
To make your future brighter
Make it stay the same

To follow all the dreams you have
Never let them go
Will surely be a sin of fate
Forever let you know

That your purpose here is not to follow
Put your strength behind
Each decision that you make
Will never leave you blind

ANTICIPATION

The anticipation of a wee one,
Was more then we could hope for.
A child being born into a world
Of siblings many.

We watched as cradles and linens
Came out to blossom a room full of joy.
As Mom and Dad held spirits high,
Our little wee one would be born.

The day came for the return of the group,
Who helped us anticipate joy.
With only one step or two out the door,
Our world would be yours.

As they walked slowly to the step of the house
That waited patiently still.
Came the little bundle of emptiness,
Our hearts stood still.

Asking where our little wee one could be,
As their arms dangled solemnly still,
As tear filled eyes of sorrow,
Looked upon we were told.

She returned from once she came,
In God's heavenly glow.
As a special angel,
To cherish, never to hold.

22

Listen, Watch, Find It Real

Sorrowful moments surrounding your tears
A season you've dreaded most of these years
Walking in circles, day and night
Searching smiles, lost, out of sight

A spark comes from heaven, group help, was found
Helping hand strength, bringing as one
Walking a journey harder than hard
Understanding feelings others cannot

End of a journey has hit as a thump
Hearts have been lowered
Our hearts took a plunge
Loneliness felt without a doubt

Met as strangers, not long ago
New lifelong friends to behold
Helping each other without a doubt
Part of the journey, happily found

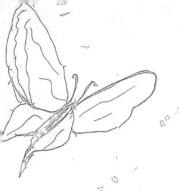

A PEARL

A pearl of darkness
A pearl of light

Can sometimes make
The stars seem bright

Outraged feelings
Love's tenderness

How often can we
Share in this

A rainbow's light
Brighten the skies

A dark cloud hovering
Over you and I

Your emotions stick to
The cage of your ribs

Like a swollen lake
That meets the ridge

Wake up to sunshine
Let everything go

Let sunshine inside
As well as outdoors

PATH OF STRENGTH

Walking our path
Interesting lives appear
Into our world of love and cheer
With doubts of progress always near

We walk into a darkened path
While lights appear as darkness stays
A world we always knew could come
Now to pass the darkened hall

A little light will show some day
Run toward it and hope it stays
As you briskly wait to see
It disappears, darkness appears

TV blares from wake till sleep
Hoping we can feel complete
Noise of people all around
Helps to shuffle feet

Now I see the clock with four
Instead I know the door is closed
God I'm begging, let it be
To bring me home, please let me see

The darkness back I stand alone
I know he'll never walk the floor
God, bring me strength until the morn
I pray the shine will soon be born

28

A SISTER'S LOVE

A heart filled with compassion,
A smile of wit and charm,
A sister's love will never leave,
Time will still move on.

Together you can move the world,
With love so strong and deep.
As we watch the years go by,
Though we seldom speak.

We'll always be there with our *strength*,
When tears of sorrow fall.
Bringing in a smile or two,
As laughter fills the hall.

A sister's love will always speak,
Louder than her words,
Love is always stronger,
Than a gesture never heard.

Today I write the feelings
I have always felt inside.
I love you, my dear sister,
With deep happiness and pride.

ANGELS

The angels whispered
The words today
They fluttered brightly
Around your head

They flew into
Your world today
Revealing your angels
On duty today

Returning to reality
As your opened eyes
Blinking I'm free
Room darkening sight

The days continue
As shortness of breath
A painful duty
Without some rest

Strength of soul
Weakness sets in
Angels come forward
Your journey begins

As peaceful lights
Approach as you lay
Rest in peace
We'll see you someday

MY LITTLE MAN

I whispered a prayer for you today,
As I watched your fragile body lay.
Wrapped in linen's so soft, so white,
Struggling with each breath, holding tight.

God gave us an angel for just a short time.
We are blessed to have known you, as we question why.
You'll be with us forever in our hearts our minds,
On the road that we travel until it's our time.

We will find you in flowers, as they bloom in the spring,
Snuggle you warmly, as the snows begin.
We will wake in the morning, as the sun forms your smile,
Our lives will be empty, our souls filled with pride.

Someday we will meet in a world far away,
Where GOD and his angels want you to play.
When that day comes, we will walk hand in hand,
Until then *good night*, my little man.

34

REMEMBERING

Remembering all the little things
Help rule our world
Love of plenty, hardships hate
Overtaking pain and strength

Looking into newborn eyes
Celebrating love of life
Knowing of its innocence
Surely, shortly lived

Damaging parts of life begin
With each breath we take
Hopefully finding wisdom
Nourishing life's regrets

Time goes on, lessons learned
Hoping better thoughts
Life embracing, newer love
As we build the chart

Every step has taken
Journeys faithful road
Into life of treasures
Always to behold

So lift a head of pride and joy
Never to regret
Steps are taken, wrong or right
Holding of your breath

Pretty smile upon your face
Gentle, soft, and sweet
Your eyes tell of your mistakes
Through everyone you meet

Shyness overwhelms the air
As someone words a lie
Your face forms a look of right
Until the moments gone

The pain you feel is very real
Hope you'll soon believe
This feeling that you have inside
Will always leave you clear

FRIENDSHIP STRENGTH

Remembering years past
In high school as we played
Remembering rides we took
In a new car as it ran

The Elm Street speeding
Through the street
Threatening a haircut make
As fellows lengths of locks
Could surely make a wig

We laughed, chased, enjoyed
Dates with fellows of other states
Walking when the car was gone
Until repairs were made

Our lives revolved of separate worlds
Our families pure and strong
Meeting far between each year
Not knowing times shortness fall

Many years will pass between
Meetings of our souls
As we walked into our lives
With memories to hold

A precious gift was given us
Friendship's strong embrace
Many years of loving words
Never to forget

WHIMSICAL VOICE

Look up to see
Outstretched wings.
Feathers of brilliant white,
Fondling the strength around
A whimsical voice.
Just listen to the
Breeze of love
That's felt all around you,
Hold on to the voice that
Can't be heard.
The profits of the sky
Look up to see,
Angels and their beauty,
You say!
You can't see!
Believe and you will,
Each morning as the sun shines,
At night in twilight as you sleep.

WALK IN SILENCE FOR TOMORROW

She walks with grace and laughter,
A golden flow among
The many people that she meets
Has brought us all as one.

No future without holding
A precious love for all
To see the glitter in her eyes,
How life has brought a song.

Her happiness surrounds us
With every waking day.
The roses that have fallen
Have glistened back in place.

The darkness never brings her down,
Her smile, how grand, complete.
A friendship that will never end,
Though we never speak.

A tale of no tomorrows,
A songbird sings the phrase,
Please let the wonders of belief
Become an inward praise.

To grieve and not remember,
A sin within itself.
Help the world remember
Her life's unselfish love.

42

GRAYNESS

Grayness overcomes the land
Where rich colors
Hang from every limb.

Colors turn to shades of white,
Grazing from the sky,
Gathering winter's harvest,
Poor man's gold.

Crystal glaziers glowing on the limbs,
Sleeping in the winds till springs awakening buds.
Early treasures of sprouting greens,
Peeking through the brown of the earth,
Muddled in the winter's thaw.

As rivers swell to a bubbling brook of passing froth,
Essence of warmer weather to come,
As tulips open with a smile,
Toward the early summer's ray of sun,
Bringing forth the smell of firewood
Burning at the camps of leisurely summer days.

Whispering winds of falling leaves,
Yellows, reds, greens,
Bringing the circle to see
Grayness overcome, turning of the trees.

44

AN ANGEL'S HAND TO GUIDE YOU

So many words are spoken,
So little time we had
To help in comfort as we heal,
A heart with tears to shed.

The angels came to visit,
Holding out their hands,
With seas of lights surrounding,
A soothing sound they had.

"Come with us," they whispered.
"You've suffered long enough.
It's time to rest your body.
Come with us, gentle one."

The time has come to look away
To find your peace above.
The tears have shed from those who love,
Yet they will understand.

So take their hands and follow.
God waits for you with pride.
Be not afraid to travel,
Guardian angels by your side.

With beauty that's unfolded,
The peace you'll find is grand,
As you are walking hand in hand
To see the Promised Land.

INSPIRATION

I read the poetry to be found
The pages not so torn

To words that mean that life is great
Or just a little childhood hate

Your words inspire also do they
Rejoice with wisdom of today

To reach the souls of those
Who can't relate

Your world was not a fairy tale told
It was of a childhood never to bold

The words that spoke of yesteryear
Have long been just a bright full year

INTERLOVELET

The internet has given you
A special life to hold.

It has carried you across the miles
To riches yet untold.

A hand to hold the memories
Of life "your magic sword."

To always see the strength
That comes within your soul.

Even though your miles away,
Find happiness and strength.

To live your life in full,
As destiny creates.

Be not afraid of challenge,
Be strong, wise, discrete.

To always know you have the strength
To make your life complete.

TWO SIDES

Two sides of a coin
One good, one not
Two faces of eve
One loving, one not

Two sides of the road
One coming, one not
Two sides of a fountain
One with beauty, one without

To many options…to many doubts
To many sorrows, to many rights
So many people, two-sided thoughts
So many feelings, too much doubts

So much anger, not enough laughter
So many accusations, not enough trust
So many words, not enough silence
So many cold handshakes, not enough love

52

WINTER'S WORLD

Time has come, footsteps
Marking of frozen snow
Cold and bitter scene
People racing, ice-covered world

Car awaiting the engines revel
Draining of the start
Shoulders shivering
Waiting to open a frozen lock

Keys refusing to gather
Strength of inner force
To open a snow-filled
Cavity of un-started warmth

As the winds continue to hollow out
New unbridled garments, unwanted cloth
Door begins to open, sigh of relief
Anticipation of sitting on a frozen leather seat

Engines start with anticipated warmth
Beginning to gather, lingering coldness
Heated excitement
Of a long winter's night thaw

As the engine becomes the focus of the noise
A sound of reviving comes within the engine's core
Turning of the sound once expected
Turns into unexpected silence

Oh my...a panic impacting the inner frozen souls
Asking for the help from his inner pores
Please, please, please, it's time to start
As fingers refuse to turn, the hand held part

"Let's try again," say a whispered prayer
Moments of anticipation, as the motor sings
Sounds of humming from the frozen engine's core
Warming seats during a winter's morning thaw

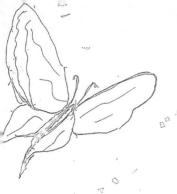

ADVENTURE

Start adventures
Begin as we wake
Up down, dressing mode
TV says I'm late

News just blared, single notes
Means no more to me
As the words are spoken
Little smirks complete

Words of wisdom, incomplete
Taking time to think
Thank you for including
One's that repeat

Rumbles, gestures, unspoken remarks
Airways filled, tension like a knife
Thinking it's the best, must be mistake
Out comes happiness in its place

Left is right, right is no
Minds bewildered, painful throws
Undecided directions, answers not
Help, help, confusion begins
Adventure stops

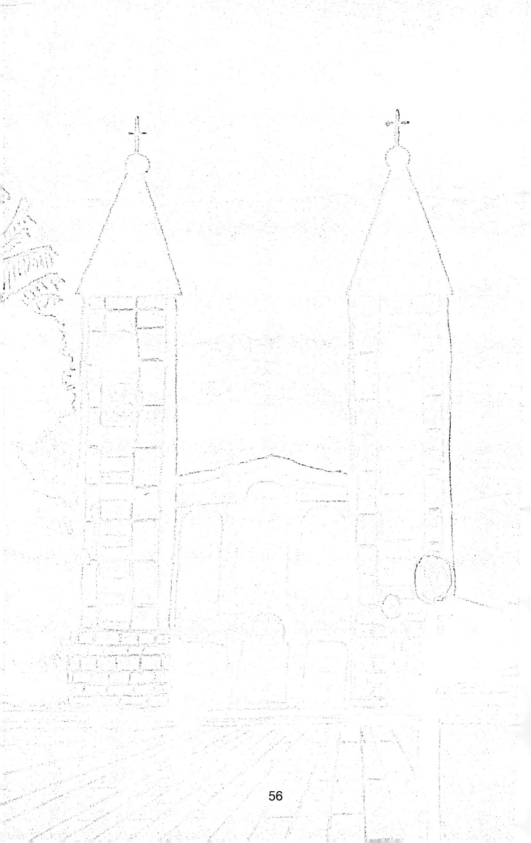

FLAMING WINGS

The sky of blue
Surrounds the flaming wings
Of beauty among us.

The golden nest of strands,
Sweeping the seas of gold
To rest upon the shadows
Of wondrous doubt.

Among the rainbows of delight,
peaceful, intriguing,
Descant with love and wonder
Within ourselves.

58

CREATURES OF MYSTERY

Rev up the motors,
Let's get underway

To search the mysteries
Of creatures through the bay

Together we will see
As far, as far can be

The beauty of these mammals
The way they ought to be

Oh, the beauty of a mother
A calf is by her side

Riding the waves of wonder
Of how they can survive

Their beauty is incredible
Their gentleness sublime

To watch is like a movie
That doesn't leave your mind

If you can find the time
To cruise with Captain Red

Please say hello for me
To the whales you'll see ahead

GADGETS AND GIZMOS

There are kitchen helpers we can't do without,
Peeling, cleaning, cutting about.
The unwanted remnants, just throw them away,
A gadget to scrap is easier that way.

A pairing knife's lovely, so tiny and sharp,
Gets into the crevices others cannot.
The peeler can shave, the smoothest of all,
With razor-sharp edges, a carrot yells, "yeeow."

So many new characters hanging around,
So many to mention without a doubt.
When looking, not finding, a gadget is lost,
Off to the market, who cares what it cost.

As long as we find one to help with the chores,
Our lives are much easier, our fingers not sore.
Thanks to the people whose mind worked so hard,
Introducing the gadgets and gizmos we find.

62

A WISH THAT CAN COME TRUE

Your angel is a special friend,
Who'll never leave your side.

Wear your angel well,
Think of him with pride.

His wings will flutter through the sky,
To form around the clouds.

If you watch him close enough,
Your face will never frown.

Your strength will come from deep within,
Although you may not know.

That life is not another game,
It means a whole lot more.

So fight real hard and find the strength,
That you will muster through.

To help your angel work,
So very hard for you.

THE OTHER DAY

I stepped into another world
the other day

A world which filled with memories
The other day

Of water bold with waves of gold
The other day

My world of beauty has long been gone
The other day

To bring back a daily task
The other day

A task that will oppress my world
The other day

Of dailyness and weeklyness
The other day

66

FROM MY HEART TO YOU

Today I found the words to say,
To tell you what my heart dismayed,
About my life, you taught me well,
To believe in what I could not tell.
Your rules weren't simple yet quite direct,
I grew up knowing to give respect.
We were of eight with one unknown,
In a childhood which has long been gone.
Our children hear the stories told,
Among the years that were so bold.
We laughed and cried with many fears.
Someday our lives would disappear
Into a world we can but share,
With siblings spread most everywhere.
Your house was firm yet very soft,
In a way you'd never really thought
Of how our strength has come from you.
Even though at times as a child we knew
That a rant and rage would never do,
But as we grew, we came across
The love we knew we'd never lost.
So be of pride to know the truth.
Your children really look at you
For strength and love that we all feel,
Inside our souls so very real.

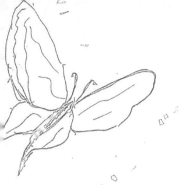

WINTER'S JOURNEY

Upon the Willow Creek they ran,
Hiding from the winds,
Blowing cold, within the snows,
Hanging limb to limb.

Where do they hide
Discomforts they are feeling?
A thought has come to my amaze,
Witnessing a planned retreat.

They scurried faster as snows lingered,
A white blanket onto a golden reddish fur.
Treat filled cheeks into the earth,
Under the trees called home.

A bungalow surface, deep below the covered soil,
Watching as they hurried into a well-made entrance,
Leading into a burrow, hoping to escape unharmed
To safety, warmth, food, resting in comfort
From winter's lingering song.

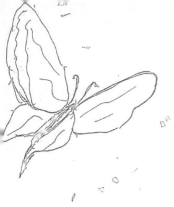

LOST CHILD

Little lost child
Among the holes

Society watch
Society hold

The crying fear
Within their minds

Will soon believe
That they can climb

Back to the place
Where they belong

Among the riches
Of their songs

The little lost child
Has just begun

To figure out
What life has done

To hold on to
The past as well

As living with
The hand that held

The love that knows
The truth that bares

Among the years
Of foster care

LIFELONG FRIEND

Remembering years past
High school as we played
Remembering the rides we took
A new car as it ran

The Elm Street speeding
Up down roads of strength
Threatening cutting hair of length
As they would despair

Laughing, catching, enjoying dates
Fellows of other states
Walking when the car was gone
Into repairing states

Lives revolving of separate worlds
Families pure and strong
Meeting far between each year
Not knowing time has gone

Many years will pass between
Encounters, friendships, loves
Remembering all the wonders
A friendship never lost

Rest in peace, my lifelong friend
Warmly in God's embrace
Smiling down upon us
Life without regrets

PROCRASTINATION RIDE

The movement of the car,
How restful it can be
To take mind off problems,
The work that ought to be.

I sit upon a cushioned seat,
How soft it is to ride.
To feel the wheels beneath you,
To see the trees passed by.

I may not feel so guilty
To leave the dishes there.
Because I cannot wash them,
The sink is just not here.

The vacuum cleaner sits upon
The rug that's stained,
Yes…let it sit forever.
I'm on a ride today.

I made the bed this morning,
A task not always done.
The accomplishment of that
Takes the guilty away from some.

This restful ride is giving
The time to contemplate.
If I can have another day,
To let this task await.

MY DREAM

Day of wonder
Day of love
Day to spend
Having Fun

A dream came true
The other day
A dream of happiness
On display

We always have
A cherished love
Material dreams
From above

Heart attack wakens numbers one
Storms of wonder song of love
Helping children learn to grow
Into masters of control

78

FRIENDLY KITCHEN

Join our hands around the room
So filled with love, hearts abloom
To follow sunrise in the dawn
Of broken hearts with cryful mourns

A helping hand a smile of soul
A pantry full, a bag to hold
Our secret is to never make
The person who has come to see
A smile, a greeting, a friendship peek

Join our hands, pray out loud
For everyone who can't somehow
See a rainbow in their life
We can help shed a light

For every human who comes forth
To nourish hold or just to talk
Believe in miracles, they come true
For all of you who see it through

A VERY SPECIAL GIFT

I sit upon a mountain trail
To heal, to reflect,
As tears of troubled past and present
Flow upon my chest.

I pray so deep within my soul,
So very far from home.
As angels voices help to sooth
The troubled voice I hold.

I listen very carefully
To a lovely melody.
As singing wings of birds in flight
Bring me to my knees.

As children walking, heads held high,
Singing faithfully.
My prayers strong within my soul,
Feeling close to thee.

A gift of love was placed upon
The sounds of tenderness.
As I open up my heart,
I thank you for this gift.

SEARCHING

Watching, watching, as they move,
Faster, faster, sliding through,
Harder than a landing post,
Brighter than the lamppost's glow.

Always watching, never seeing,
Movements holding true to form.
Holding onto different pages,
Never truly feeling strong.

Shouting, wishing, painfully watching,
Anticipating every move.
Missed again, shouting, roaring,
Feelings can't complete the mood.

Floating into unknown places,
Hoping we can watch the glow,
As the whispering sound around us
Brings us to a newfound world.

FEELINGS

Among the raindrops you may find
The tears of sorrow hidden.

An ice cream cone cannot suffice
The feeling that's within him.

So look real deep to find the key
That may unravel life.

To touch the hidden anger
He may not want alive.

The anger may just surface,
Unwillingly someday.

To show the true beginnings
Of lives hidden away.

The secret to the doorway
May never cease to find.

The sorrow that's within him,
A mask that seems so blind.

To the laughter we can see
Among the smile so wide.

Search within his eyes,
And you may realize.

The laughter you are hearing
Is nothing but a lie.

Of dreams he wants to fondle
With memories erased.

His laughter then will be
Of trueness, not of fake.

To show the world he recovered
From faces of the day.

ABOUT THE AUTHOR

Born in New Hampshire, Jeannine Gingras has always called this state her home. She has traveled to many places like Italy, Medjugoria, Bosnia, Croatia, and among many states of the Union. She was married at the age of nineteen to her wonderful husband, Robert. They were married forty-seven years before God brought him home. Jeannine and Robert have three wonderful children—Derrick (Brandi), Daniel (Susannah), and Doreen (Jamey). They gave them nine beautiful grandchildren and four great-grandchildren. Jeannine had been writing poetry since high school, using many life experiences to create.

Jeannine's husband was her best critic, listening to every word (he didn't care for poetry). He was a great audience. She was finally convinced by her youngest sibling, Linda, that she should share her words. Jeannine also wants to thank everyone in her life with encouraging words of wisdom in finally finding the courage. Most of all, she thanks God for all the inspirational words and blessings and the gift to create.

She does pray that they will help at least one person reading them. May God bless them with peace and prosperity.

CPSIA information can be obtained
at www.ICGtesting.com
Printed in the USA
BVHW041304020522
635891BV00004B/40